HABITAT H

LANDFILLS

By Greg Roza

Gareth Stevens
Publishing

Please visit our website, www.garethstevens.com. For a free color catalog of all our high-quality books, call toll free 1-800-542-2595 or fax 1-877-542-2596.

Library of Congress Cataloging-in-Publication Data

Roza, Greg.
Landfills / by Greg Roza.
  p. cm. — (Habitat havoc)
Includes index.
ISBN 978-1-4339-9923-9 (pbk.)
ISBN 978-1-4339-9924-6 (6-pack)
ISBN 978-1-4339-9921-5 (library binding)
1. Refuse and refuse disposal — Juvenile literature. 2. Sanitary landfills — Juvenile literature. I. Roza, Greg. II. Title.
TD792.R69 2014
363.728—dc23

First Edition

Published in 2014 by
Gareth Stevens Publishing
111 East 14th Street, Suite 349
New York, NY 10003

Copyright © 2014 Gareth Stevens Publishing

Designer: Andrea Davison-Bartolotta
Editor: Kristen Rajczak

Photo credits: Cover, p. 1 iStockphoto/Thinkstock; p. 5 Steve Dunwell/Photolibrary/Getty Images; p. 7 Kirsanov Valeriy Vladimirovich/Shutterstock.com; p. 8 Hulton Archive/Getty Images; p. 9 Jacques Boyer/ Roger Viollet/Getty Images; p. 11 Bill Pierce/Time & Life Pictures/Getty Images; p. 13 (both) oleksa/ Shutterstock.com; p. 14 Ari N/Shutterstock.com; p. 15 Britta Gustafson/Wikimedia Commons; p. 16 Christophe Simon/AFP/Getty Images; p. 17 (both) Antonio Scorza/AFP/Getty Images; p. 18 federicofoto/ Shutterstock.com; p. 19 (inset) BSIP/UIG via Getty Images; p. 19 (main) Daniel Acker/Bloomberg via Getty Images; pp. 20–21 Joe Traver/Liaison/Getty Images; pp. 22–23 Buffalutheran/Wikimedia Commons; p. 23 (inset) EPA/Wikimedia Commons; p. 25 courtesy of Green Group Holdings; p. 26 Dave Pape/ Wikimedia Commons; p. 27 Becky Hayes/Shutterstock.com; pp. 28–29 Walter Zerla/Cultura/Getty Images.

Printed in the United States of America

CPSIA compliance information: Batch #CW14GS: For further information contact Gareth Stevens, New York, New York at 1-800-542-2595.

Contents

Words in the glossary appear in **bold** type the first time they are used in the text.

MUCH ADO ABOUT SOLID WASTE

Hopefully you understand how important it is to recycle and reuse items instead of throwing them away. Reducing the amount of garbage we throw away is an easy way to do our part in protecting the **environment**.

But some of the trash we throw away can't be recycled. This "solid waste" contains anything from banana peels to harmful chemicals. Most of the time, solid waste is thrown into a hole in the ground and covered with dirt! Landfills are an unfortunate but necessary step in managing solid waste. However, careless landfill practices have caused great harm to **habitats** around the world.

What's in Solid Waste?

Just about anything we throw away in our homes is solid waste. It also includes paints and paint cans, motor oil, car parts, furniture, construction materials, kitchen waste, and many other gross things. In other words, solid waste is anything that's discarded, or thrown away. Many of these things are very bad for the environment.

Landfills can take away animals' habitats and harm their surroundings enough to cause illness or even death.

5

DUMPS AND DISEASES

From the time humans first started living in communities, they've had to find ways to deal with solid waste. As urban centers grew, many lacked proper waste management practices. In some towns and cities, people simply threw their trash—often including human waste—out the window! The filth attracted pests, such as the rats whose fleas spread the **plague**.

The first **municipal** waste management programs helped clean up cities, but they simply moved the problem elsewhere: the municipal dump. Dumping and burning garbage are very bad for people and equally bad for the environment.

Leaking Leachate!

Mountains of garbage in a dump contain many substances, including liquids. These liquids mix together as they seep down into the ground. Rainwater washes over solid waste and creates more liquid. This toxic mixture of liquids is called leachate. Modern landfills must take steps to keep it contained.

Dumping is the oldest form of waste management, and it's still used around the world today.

By the late 1800s, people in towns and cities urged local governments to do something. The first waste management programs had trash burned or used horse-drawn carts to haul it to a municipal dump. Some dumped it in the sea. Some cities mixed garbage with dirt and rocks, and used it to fill in swamps. Although these methods seemed fine to people back then, they caused great damage to the environment and disrupted countless habitats.

The first landfills appeared around 1920. Many were simply deep holes that gradually filled up with garbage. However, an ever-growing public concern for the environment resulted in gradual improvements.

DON'T FEED RATS

That Stinks!

A study of one North Carolina community found that when the stink from the nearby landfill got worse, more eye, nose, throat, and breathing problems occurred in residents! That's because the increased odor was connected to a rise in a toxic gas called hydrogen sulfide, which is produced by garbage breaking down at landfills.

Did early cities smell like rotting garbage? Some of that was air pollution that could harm the health of people and animals nearby!

By the 1960s, many existing landfills in the United States were overflowing and contained **hazardous** materials. People began wondering if old landfills were dangerous to communities and the environment. Some landfills made headlines when those living near them started to get really sick, and this led to public anger. Once again, people urged the government to do something.

In 1976, Congress passed an act that increased the federal government's role in waste management. Local and federal governments examined ways to make landfills safer for people and Earth. Thanks to the US Environmental Protection Agency (EPA), today's landfills are scientifically designed to protect the environment—but how successful are they?

Hurray for RCRA!

The Resource **Conservation** and Recovery Act (RCRA) is the main federal law governing the disposal of solid waste and hazardous substances. The standards it sets are designed to protect human health. RCRA also ensures that wastes are disposed of in an environmentally friendly way by permitting the EPA to follow hazardous wastes "from cradle to grave"—from when they are created to when they are recycled or disposed of.

In the early 1970s, metals and other hazardous materials were disposed of in the Lipari Landfill in New Jersey. Later, a study showed that the toxic dump caused low birth weights in babies born to families that lived close to the dump, especially in the years when the hazardous waste disposal was highest.

protest of Lipari Landfill

11

THE LIFE OF A LANDFILL

Well-designed landfills **isolate** solid waste from the environment. The most important part is the bottom layer, or liner. This includes a layer of **compacted** clay, covered with a thick, strong plastic. Some liners don't use both.

Over the bottom liner, workers place garbage in sections called cells. This is where bulldozers tear up, crush, and squash garbage all day. At the end of the day, the fresh garbage is covered with 6 to 12 inches (15 to 30 cm) of dirt. This covers the smell and keeps pests away, which is why these landfills were first known as sanitary, or clean, landfills.

Landmark Landfill

The Fresno Sanitary Landfill was the first sanitary landfill. It opened in 1937. For the next 50 years, the residents of Fresno, California, sent their garbage there. Today, the site is covered with soil and light grass grows on it. It's also on the National Register of Historic Places!

new dump site

Even when landfills are constructed properly, leachate may leak into the groundwater, causing dangerous toxins to **contaminate** streams, rivers, and even drinking water.

Landfills vary in size. Some are enormous. Puente Hills Landfill was the largest active landfill in the United States until it closed in 2013. Since opening in 1957, it received almost 130 million tons (118 million mt) of solid waste. It's now the height of a 40-story building!

Once it's full, a landfill must be closed. It's sealed with a cap, which is a layer of heavy plastic. Then the site is covered with about 2 feet (61 cm) of compacted soil. A layer of topsoil allows grass and other small plants to grow. This stops rain and wind from wearing the soil away.

Kinds of Landfills

Puente Hills is a municipal landfill, which is the final resting place of everyday garbage from homes, businesses, and schools. A construction and **demolition** (C&D) landfill accepts materials used in construction, such as wood, glass, metals, bricks, and plastic. Industrial landfills receive waste from factories and mines. Many of those materials are highly toxic.

C&D waste site

Landfills like this one in Puente Hills, California, pose pollution problems even after they close. The trash in them doesn't break down for a long time, which means the environmental risk also remains.

15

BAD, BAD LANDFILLS!

Sanitary landfills were introduced in the 1930s to reduce the smell and disease-carrying pests caused by open dumps. They weren't exactly designed with the environment in mind. People were, at least temporarily, safe from garbage. However, it took a heavy toll on the natural world.

Once a landfill closes, the environment around it must be **monitored** for years to make sure the landfill is doing its job. Broken caps and liners result in a black, bubbly liquid leaking into the ground. This can poison nearby water sources and kill local plants and animals. The leaks are plugged with compacted dirt, but it shows that landfills will always be a threat to local habitats.

Gramacho Garden

The Jardim Gramacho Landfill in Rio de Janeiro, Brazil, was built near the once-beautiful Guanabara Bay. The site wasn't prepared with a liner. Since 1978, fluids made by rotting waste have seeped into the ground and the bay. This has made the water unsafe for people and animals.

While it's smart to monitor the air, water, and soil around a closed landfill, it can be costly to do so.

trash in Guanabara Bay

17

Natural processes can damage a landfill's liner and cap. Wind, water, and ice can cause them to break down. Plant roots, if they grow deep enough, can pierce the cap. So can burrowing animals. Cave-ins inside a landfill can cause cracks in the liner and cap. Landfills are monitored carefully to watch for these things, but we can't see damage that's underground. That's why workers must also monitor the soil and groundwater around a closed landfill for many years.

Landfills can pose risks to the environment when they leak. However, some landfills are more dangerous because of the toxic items placed in them.

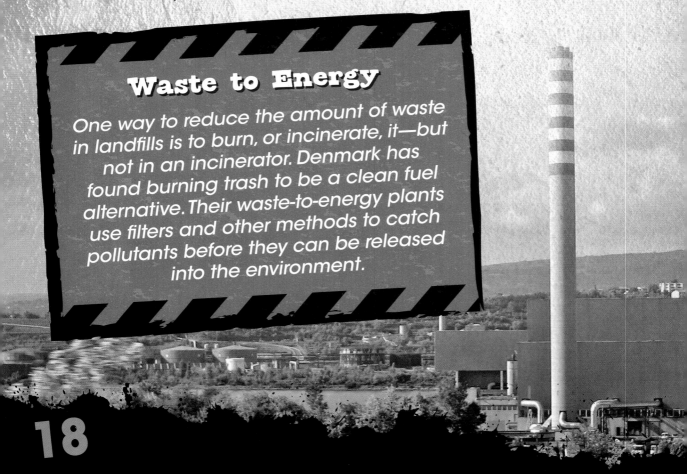

Waste to Energy

One way to reduce the amount of waste in landfills is to burn, or incinerate, it—but not in an incinerator. Denmark has found burning trash to be a clean fuel alternative. Their waste-to-energy plants use filters and other methods to catch pollutants before they can be released into the environment.

For centuries, towns and cities have incinerated garbage to reduce the amount placed in dumps and landfills. This puts harmful chemicals into the air. Also, filling landfills with the ash from incinerated garbage actually makes the leachate thicker and more toxic.

garbage incinerator

TRAGEDY AT LOVE CANAL

Love Canal—a former community in Niagara Falls, New York—showed the world just how dangerous landfills can be. Part of a canal was dug, but by 1910, the site was abandoned. In the 1920s, this canal was used as a landfill. From 1942 to 1953, the Hooker Chemical Company buried about 22,000 tons (20,000 mt) of chemical waste in the landfill.

After the landfill had been closed and covered with dirt, the site was sold to the city of Niagara Falls for $1. A new school and neighborhood were built near the covered landfill. It was just a matter of time before **tragedy** struck.

Taking Responsibility

The Hooker Chemical Company sold the land to Niagara Falls for $1 and warned of the dangerous chemicals in the contract. They did this to avoid being sued in the future. However, state and federal governments "persuaded" the company to contribute $129 million to the cleanup process.

Heavy rain and snow in 1975 and 1976 caused huge drums of chemicals to surface at the landfill.

In the early 1970s, residents of the Love Canal community began noticing strange smells. Some reported an oily liquid leaking into their basements. It wasn't long before studies showed that numerous chemicals from the landfill had contaminated the soil, water, and air.

The toxic chemicals caused **cancer** in residents and **birth defects** in babies, but it was equally damaging to the environment. Nearby creeks were contaminated; it wasn't safe to eat fish from them for years. A cap was placed over the location, and a drainage system was installed. However, dangerous chemicals are still buried there, and a large area is still fenced off to protect the public.

Superfund

News of Love Canal shocked and horrified the nation. In 1980, the US government passed the Comprehensive Environmental Response, Compensation, and Liability Act, better known as "Superfund." This law was designed to provide money for cleaning up toxic waste sites such as Love Canal. The money comes from the chemical companies that cause these problems.

More than 400 chemicals were found in the air, water, and soil around Love Canal.

DANGER
HAZARDOUS AREA
UNAUTHORIZED
PERSONNEL
KEEP OUT

NEW YORK STATE
ENVIRONMENTAL
CONSERVATION
1-800-42-9296

warning sign at
Love Canal

MODERN LANDFILLS

Because of the tragedies that occurred at Love Canal and similar sites, the federal government finally made strict landfill laws to protect people and the environment. One of the greatest improvements is the use of leachate collection systems. While preparing a landfill, the bottom is designed to guide leachate to a low point. There, the liquids are collected using a system of pipes buried in sand and gravel that lead to a collection pond. This system keeps the soil and groundwater from being contaminated by leachate.

Modern landfills are also designed with storm water drainage systems. These carry extra water away from the site so it doesn't contribute to leachate, too.

Collecting Methane

Rotting garbage and leachate create waste gases, including methane. This gas is dangerous to people and is one of the gases that causes global climate change. Modern landfills have methane collection systems similar to leachate collection systems. In the past, many landfills simply burned the methane so it didn't harm the environment. Today, most landfills use the methane to create electricity.

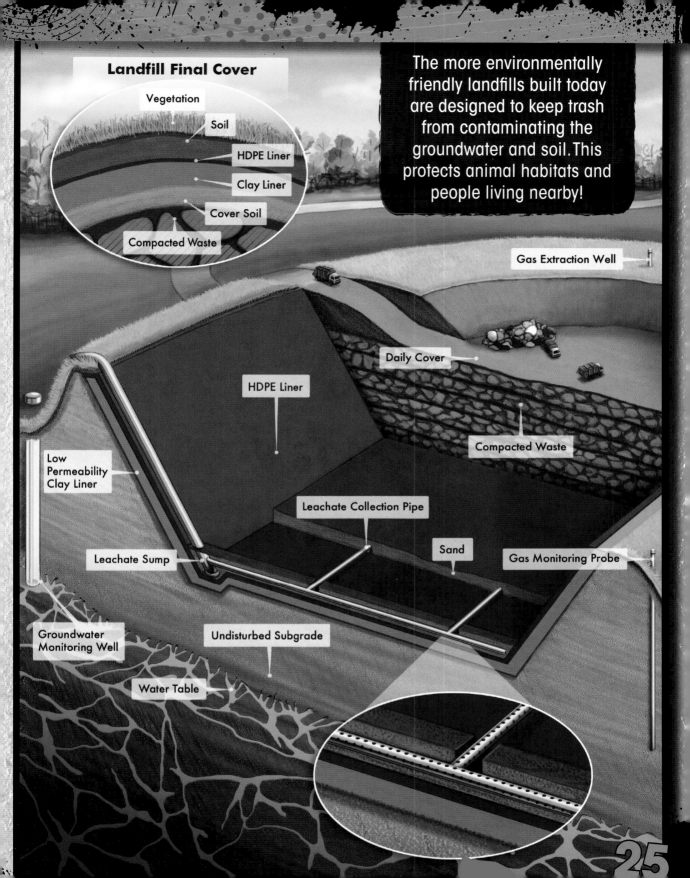

Landfills in the United States require hundreds of acres. Experts study the soil and make sure the rock is watertight. It can't have any cracks in it that might let chemicals flow through. Landfills can't be built near rivers, streams, or wetlands. The flow of water in the area is studied to prevent leachate from reaching groundwater. Scientists also study local plants and animals to make sure the landfill won't disrupt fragile habitats or any **endangered species**.

Once a landfill closes, efforts are made to return the area to a natural state. If all goes well, both plants and animals may return to the area. Some closed landfills have even been turned into parks and nature preserves.

Tifft Nature Preserve

Just a few miles south of downtown Buffalo, New York, Tifft Nature Preserve is home to deer, marsh animals, fish, and many kinds of birds. Tifft also offers programs to help educate people about conservation and the environment. This 264-acre (107 ha) nature preserve was built on top of a closed landfill!

Canada goose at Tifft Nature Preserve

A nature preserve is a place where the land, plants, animals, and other natural resources are protected from harm.

STILL A PROBLEM

Every state has Superfund cleanup sites, and many of those sites are landfills. Although cleaned sites are removed from the list, new sites are added every year. Even now, after tragedies such as Love Canal, landfills around the world still accept dangerous wastes, including electronics, chemicals, and toxic waste.

Thanks to hardworking scientists, modern landfills do all they can to protect plants, animals, and Earth itself. But no landfill is perfect, and contamination still happens. US solid waste laws might be strict, but other countries continue to dump toxic waste in overcrowded landfills. What do you think: How can we keep habitats safe from landfills?

Not Just Trash

In 2013, three coal power plants were fined for environmental issues caused by the ash they disposed of in Maryland landfills. Toxic chemicals found in coal ash were contaminating the groundwater and were found in the bodies of fish in nearby streams! One of the landfills that took in coal ash was said to have chronic, or long-lasting, pollution leakage.

Landfills are necessary. But how would you feel if one opened up near where you live?

29

Glossary

birth defect: a problem a person is born with

cancer: a disease caused by the uncontrolled growth of cells in the body

compact: to force close together

conservation: the care of the natural world

contaminate: to pollute something

demolition: the act of working with explosives to destroy things

endangered species: one kind of plant or animal that is in danger of dying out

environment: the conditions that surround a living thing and affect the way it lives

habitat: the natural place where a plant or animal lives

hazardous: very dangerous

isolate: to separate something from its surroundings

monitor: to watch the progress of something over a period of time

municipal: relating to a town or city, or its government

plague: a deadly sickness that once spread rapidly in unclean cities

tragedy: an event that causes widespread suffering or destruction

For More Information

Books

Amsel, Sheri. *The Everything Kids' Environment Book.* Avon, MA: Adams Media, 2007.

Latham, Donna. *Garbage: Investigate What Happens When You Throw It Out.* White River Junction, VT: Nomad Press, 2011.

Wilcox, Charlotte. *Earth-Friendly Waste Management.* Minneapolis, MN: Lerner, 2009.

Websites

How Landfills Work
science.howstuffworks.com/environmental/green-science/landfill.htm
Explore modern landfills from the liner up!

Reduce, Reuse, Recycle
kids.niehs.nih.gov/explore/reduce/
Now that you know how bad landfills really are for the environment, use this site to learn more about recycling!

Superfund
www.epa.gov/superfund
Learn more about Superfund and how it helps keep the environment safe from toxic waste spills.

Index